DAY HIKES IN
BOULDER
COLORADO

by Robert Stone

Photographs by Robert Stone
Published by:
Day Hike Books, Inc.
114 South Hauser Box 865
Red Lodge, MT 59068
Layout & Design: Paula Doherty
Copyright 1997
Library of Congress Catalog Card Number: 96-96517

Distributed by:
ICS Books, Inc.
1370 E. 86th Place
Merrillville, IN 46410
1-800-541-7323
Fax 1-800-336-8334

TABLE OF CONTENTS

THE HIKES

About the Hikes

Colorado is known for the majestic Rocky Mountains that divide the North American continent. Running north and south, the Colorado Rocky Mountains contain 75 percent of all the land above 10,000 feet in the continental United States, including 1,000 peaks rising over 10,000 feet and 53 peaks rising over 14,000 feet. Forty percent of Colorado—over 23 million acres—is public land. 600,000 acres are designated to the state's 11 national parks, while national forests encompass 14 million acres. Colorado also has 37 state parks, 222 wildlife areas, and 25 designated wilderness areas. More than 100 rivers flow through the state, including the headwaters of four major rivers—the Arkansas, Colorado, Platt, and Rio Grande. There are 8,000 miles of streams, 2,000 lakes and reservoirs, thousands of miles of hiking trails, and hundreds of campgrounds. The Rocky Mountains are home to bear, moose, elk, deer, antelope, big horn sheep, and mountain goats. Needless to say, outdoor recreation in Colorado is a way of life.

The Day Hikes guide to Boulder, Colorado, focuses on scenic day hikes of various lengths. All of the hikes are in or around Boulder. This college town sits nestled in the foothills of the Rocky Mountains, 30 miles northwest of Denver.

The easy access to hiking in Boulder is amazing. Within the city limits of this outdoor-oriented town are more than 170 acres of neighborhood parks and 94 acres of community parks. On the edges of town are thousands of acres of open space and hundreds of miles of trails. Chautauqua Park will take you to the base of the flatiron rock formations, an impressive landmark in Boulder that is popular with rock climbers and hikers. Boulder Mountain Park and Flagstaff Mountain, overlooking the city, encompass 33,000 acres with 100 miles of hiking trails. Whether rock climbing, biking, fishing, horseback riding, golfing, river rafting, kayaking, or hiking, Boulder is an outdoor paradise. My goal is to share some of these hikes with you and others, providing visitors as well as locals easy access to the backcountry.

A trip to Boulder would not be complete without also spending some time strolling through the Pearl Street Mall, a historically-preserved, four-block walking mall in the heart of the city. Musicians, magicians, jugglers, and other entertainers perform along this outdoor mall lined with cafes, shops, galleries, and restaurants.

The major access road to all these hikes is Broadway, which runs north and south through Boulder and intersects with each key crossroad. These hikes are detailed on United States Geological Survey topo maps and local hiking maps that can be purchased at most area sporting goods stores.

All of these hikes require easy to moderate effort and are timed at a leisurely rate. If you wish to hike faster or go further, set your own pace accordingly. As I hike, I enjoy looking at clouds, rocks, wildflowers, streams, vistas, and any other subtle pleasures of nature. While this adds to the time, it also adds to the experience.

As for attire and equipment, tennis shoes, as opposed to hiking boots, are fine for any of these hikes. Although Colorado's summer weather is usually warm and sunny, it is frequently unpredictable. Afternoon thundershowers are common. Layered clothing, a rain poncho, sunscreen, a hat, and drinking water are recommended. Pack a lunch for a picnic at scenic outlooks, streams, or wherever you find the best spot.

Enjoy your hike!

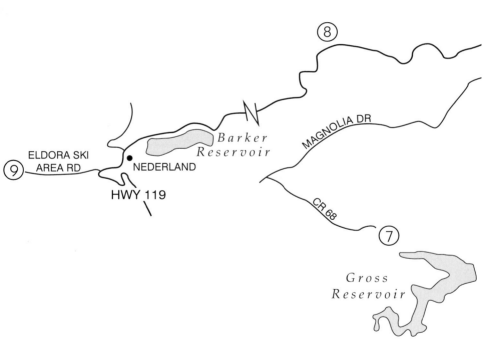

⑧

MAGNOLIA DR

Barker
Reservoir

ELDORA SKI
AREA RD

⑨

NEDERLAND

HWY 119

CR 68

⑦

Gross
Reservoir

MAP OF

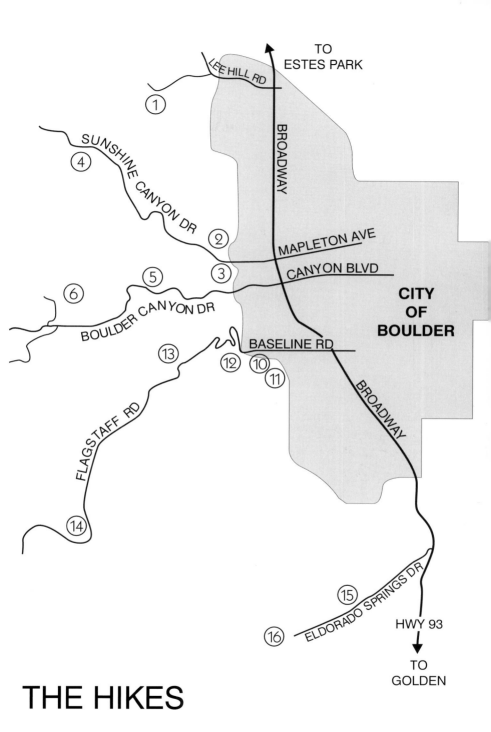

THE HIKES

Hike 1
Anne U. White Trail

Hiking Distance: 3 miles round trip
Hiking Time: 1.5 hours
Elevation Gain: 300 feet
Topo: U.S.G.S. Boulder

Summary of hike: Of all the hikes in this book, this one is Chester's favorite, my dog and walking companion. The hike follows Fourmile Canyon Creek to a waterfall and the trail end. There are over twenty creek crossings, numerous cascades, small waterfalls, pools, fantastic rock formations covered with orange lichen, and a natural rock bridge (photo on page 19).

Driving directions: From downtown Boulder, drive 3 miles north on Broadway to Lee Hill Road and turn left. Continue 1 mile to Wagonwheel Gap Road and turn left again. Drive 1.1 mile to the unpaved, unmarked Pinto Drive, with a posted "Dead End" sign on the left. (This road is located just past Bow Mountain Road.) Turn left and continue 0.2 miles to the end of the road.

Hiking directions: The trailhead is located at the end of the road. The trail gently gains elevation alongside Fourmile Canyon Creek. All of the stream crossings are easy. Some use rocks as stepping stones, and others you will just jump across. At 1.5 miles is a waterfall and pool. The area is surrounded with rock outcroppings. This is our turnaround spot. To return, follow the same trail back to the trailhead.

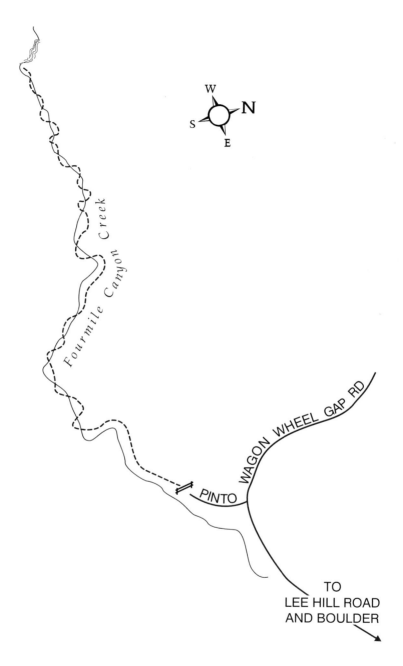

Fourmile Canyon Creek

WAGON WHEEL GAP RD

PINTO

TO
LEE HILL ROAD
AND BOULDER

ANNE U. WHITE TRAIL

Hike 2
Mount Sanitas Valley Trail

Hiking Distance: 2 miles round trip
Hiking Time: 1.5 hours
Elevation Gain: 400 feet
Topo: U.S.G.S. Boulder

Summary of hike: This hike follows a well-maintained trail in a grassy, gently-sloping valley at the base of Sunshine Canyon. To the east are views of Boulder and the eastern plains. To the west are the rock formations of Mount Sanitas rising up from the valley floor. Access to this trail is only minutes from downtown.

Driving directions: From downtown Boulder, drive north on Broadway to Mapleton Avenue. Turn left and continue 0.8 miles to a well-marked parking area on the right side.

Hiking directions: From the parking area, walk past the pavilion and cross the bridge over a creek. The trailhead begins here. A sign will direct you straight ahead to Mount Sanitas Valley. After 100 yards, take the trail to the left, and continue up the valley. A short distance up the trail is the Dakota Ridge Trail junction to the right. Stay on the Mount Sanitas Valley Trail, however, to the second Dakota Ridge Trail sign, located near the head of the valley. Take a right here, and return along the spine of this rocky ridge trail, completing the loop. Follow the main trail to the left and back to the trailhead.

For a steeper, more advanced trail, continue on the Mount Sanitas Valley Trail without returning on the Dakota Ridge Trail. The Mount Sanitas Trail climbs up red sandstone rock formations to the east ridge of Mount Sanitas and loops back to the parking area. This loop is three miles in length.

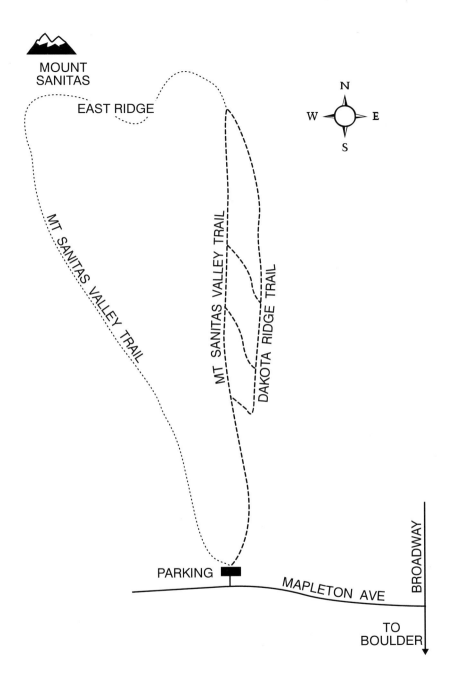

MOUNT SANITAS

Hike 3
Red Rocks Loop

Hiking Distance: 1.5 miles round trip
Hiking Time: 1 hour
Elevation Gain: 400 feet
Topo: U.S.G.S. Boulder

Summary of hike: This trail leads to a spectacular red sandstone outcropping of rocks (photo on page 19). Take the time to walk around, climb on, and marvel at these rock formations. From the Red Rocks are great views of Boulder and the eastern plains.

Driving directions: From downtown Boulder, drive north on Broadway to Mapleton Avenue. Turn left and drive one mile to the parking area on the left side of the road.

Hiking directions: From the parking lot, walk up the wooden steps and cross over the stream. Follow the trail to the Red Rocks outcropping. At the first trail junction, go left and begin the loop around these rocks. After exploring the rocks, continue down the trail clockwise and back to the trailhead.

Although this hike begins at the base of Sunshine Canyon on Mapleton Avenue, it may also be picked up on the west end of Pearl Street at Settlers Park.

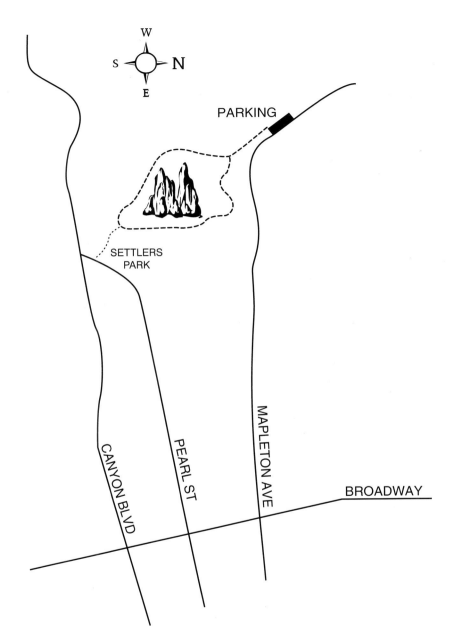

RED ROCKS LOOP

Hike 4
Pines-to-Peak Loop
Bald Mountain

Hiking Distance: 1 mile round trip
Hiking Time: 30 minutes
Elevation Gain: 240 feet
Topo: U.S.G.S. Boulder

Summary of hike: The Bald Mountain Loop is located in the 108-acre Bald Mountain Scenic Park. The mountain is aptly named as few trees survive on its 7,160-foot summit. Before ascending to the peak, however, the area is a Douglas fir and ponderosa pine parkland. The park is carpeted with a variety of grasses, shrubs, and meadows richly sprinkled with wildflowers. Along the trail are picnic sites and tables. At the summit are sweeping views of Indian Peaks and the Continental Divide to the west, the Flatirons and Flagstaff Mountain to the south, and the foothills and plains to the east.

Driving directions: From downtown Boulder, drive north on Broadway to Mapleton Avenue. Turn left on Mapleton and continue 4.8 miles to a well-marked parking area on the left. After leaving the city limits, Mapleton Avenue becomes Sunshine Canyon Drive.

Hiking directions: From the parking area, follow the well-defined trail to the south, past the picnic tables. The trail soon takes a sharp right turn to a junction. This begins the loop. Take the right fork, the Pines-to-Peak Loop Trail. A quarter mile ahead, the trail makes a wide turn to the left, through the forest to a sitting bench at the summit. From the summit, the trail curves to the left again along the northeast ridge of Bald Mountain. A short distance ahead, the path curves and descends to the right, back to the junction. Return to the picnic and parking area.

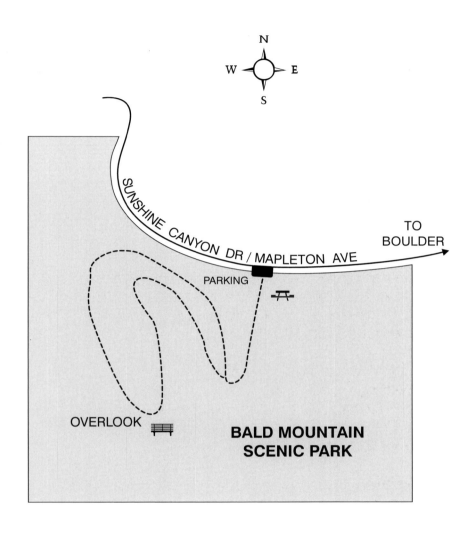

PINES-TO-PEAK LOOP

Hike 5
Boulder Creek Trail

Hiking Distance: 2.5 miles round trip
Hiking Time: 1 hour
Elevation Gain: 200 feet
Topo: U.S.G.S. Boulder

Summary of hike: This popular paved trail parallels Boulder Creek and is enjoyed by bikers, hikers, and joggers. Although the trail begins east of Boulder, our hike starts along the last and most dramatic portion of the trail, from Point O' Rocks to Fourmile Canyon (photo on page 22). Canyon cliffs are prominent along this stretch of the trail.

Driving directions: Starting from Broadway in downtown Boulder, drive 2 miles west up Canyon Boulevard to the parking area on the right side of the road by a large rock outcropping, the Elephant Buttresses.

Hiking directions: From the parking area, cross the bridge over Boulder Creek and follow the trail up canyon. The trail crosses underneath the highway and ends just past Fourmile Canyon Drive. To return, follow the path back to the parking area. Beginning the hike at the corner of Broadway and Canyon Boulevard will extend the length of the hike up to four extra miles round trip.

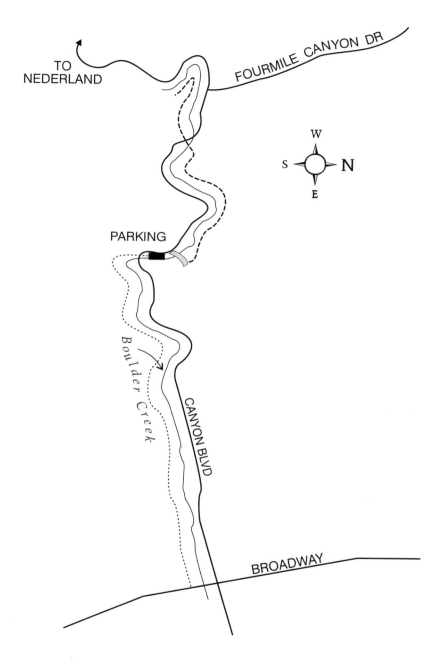

BOULDER CREEK TRAIL

Bridge crossing Boulder Creek to Lost Lake - Hike 9

Northwest Arm of Gross Reservoir - Hike 7

Cascade and pool at Fourmile Canyon Creek - Hike 1

The Red Rocks - Hike 3

Hike 6
Canyon Loop Trail
Betasso Preserve

Hiking Distance: 2.75 miles round trip
Hiking Time: 1.5 hours
Elevation Gain: 550 feet
Topo: U.S.G.S. Boulder

Summary of hike: The 773-acre Betasso Preserve is located between Boulder Canyon and Fourmile Canyon. The Canyon Loop Trail traverses grassy meadows, ravines, a small stream, and stands of ponderosa pine and Douglas fir trees. The ruins of the old McDonald homestead cabin are in the meadows.

Driving directions: Starting from Broadway in downtown Boulder, drive 5.2 miles west up the winding Canyon Boulevard to Sugarloaf Road on the right—turn right. (Canyon Boulevard turns into Boulder Canyon Drive after leaving the city limits.) Continue 0.9 miles to Betasso Road—turn right. A sign is posted at this turn. Drive 0.5 miles to the trailhead parking entrance on the left by the "Betasso Preserve" sign. Turn left and park in the lot 0.1 mile ahead.

Hiking directions: From the trailhead at the far end of the parking lot, follow the path to the right, hiking the loop clockwise. At 0.5 miles is a posted trail junction. Take the footpath to the right. The path winds gently downward into Fourmile Canyon to two forested ravines and a stream. Past the stream, the trail begins looping back, gaining elevation as it winds back to the picnic area and unpaved road. Follow the road a short distance to the right back to the parking area.

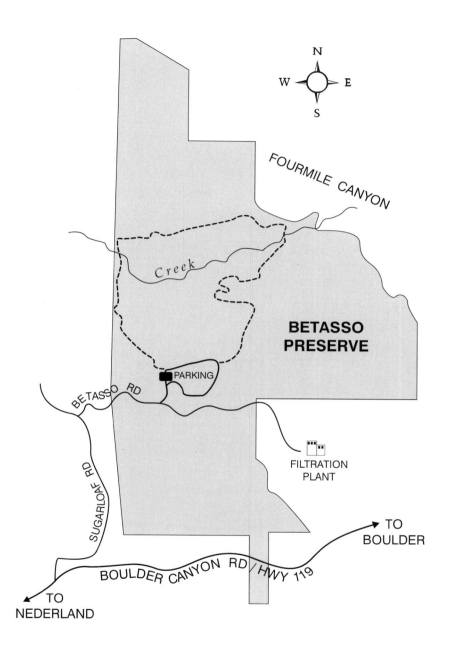

CANYON LOOP TRAIL

Boulder Falls and North Boulder Creek - Hike 8

Bridge over Boulder Creek - Hike 5

Waterfall and pool in Forsythe Canyon - Hike 7

The Flatirons from Enchanted Mesa Trail - Hike 11

Hike 7
Forsythe Canyon Creek Trail

Hiking Distance: 2.5 miles round trip
Hiking Time: 1.5 hours
Elevation Gain: 400 feet
Topo: U.S.G.S. Tungsten

Summary of hike: This hike is lightly traveled and is a gem. The Forsythe Canyon Creek Trail parallels Forsythe Creek to a beautiful waterfall and pool (photo on page 23). Along the way, the stream gently cascades over rocks. The trail ends at a secluded arm of Gross Reservoir (photo on page 18). In August, ripe raspberries are abundant.

Driving directions: Starting from Broadway in downtown Boulder, drive 5 miles west up Canyon Boulevard to Magnolia Road on the left. The road is well marked with posted signs on both sides of the highway. Turn left and drive 6.6 miles to CR 68. CR 68 is also well marked and is located 0.8 miles past Forsythe Road. Continue 2 miles to Forest Service Road 359 on the right. Turn right and park.

Hiking directions: The trailhead is not marked, but from the parking area, follow the jeep trail downhill. Within four minutes, the jeep trail curves sharply to the right. A posted foot trail leads to the left. Take the foot trail down to the stream and cross the bridge. Follow the path downstream, paralleling Forsythe Creek. The waterfall is located one mile from the trailhead. From the falls, take the trail to the left, up and over the boulders. The trail leads away from the waterfall, then curves back to the pool at the base of the falls. From the pool, continue down the main trail another three minutes to the northwest arm of Gross Reservoir. To return, follow the same trail back to the trailhead.

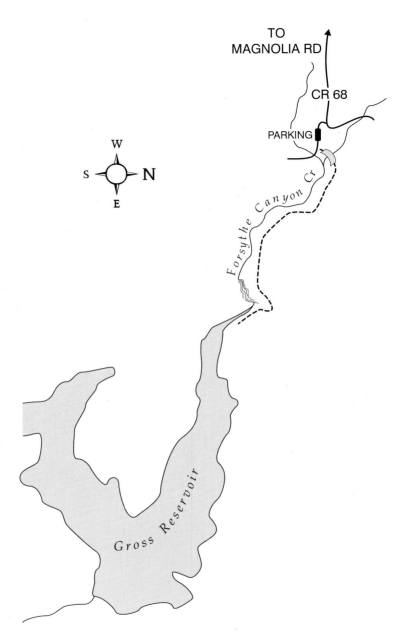

FORSYTHE CANYON
CREEK TRAIL

Hike 8
Boulder Falls

Hiking Distance: 0.25 miles round trip
Hiking Time: 15 minutes
Elevation Gain: 50 feet
Topo: U.S.G.S. Gold Hill

Summary of hike: This is a short hike to a magnificent 40-foot waterfall (cover photo). The rock surrounding this hike, called Boulder Creek granodiorite, was formed 1.7 billion years ago. The trail follows the whitewater of North Boulder Creek to the falls (photo on page 22).

Driving directions: Starting from Broadway in downtown Boulder, drive 8.6 miles west up the curving Canyon Boulevard to the parking area on the left side of the road. Canyon Boulevard turns into Boulder Canyon Drive (Highway 119) at the outskirts of town.

Hiking directions: From the parking area, cross the highway to the trailhead. The trail is mostly rock steps which parallel North Boulder Creek to the base of the falls. There are a variety of places off the path to see or photograph the falls and creek. Return along the same route.

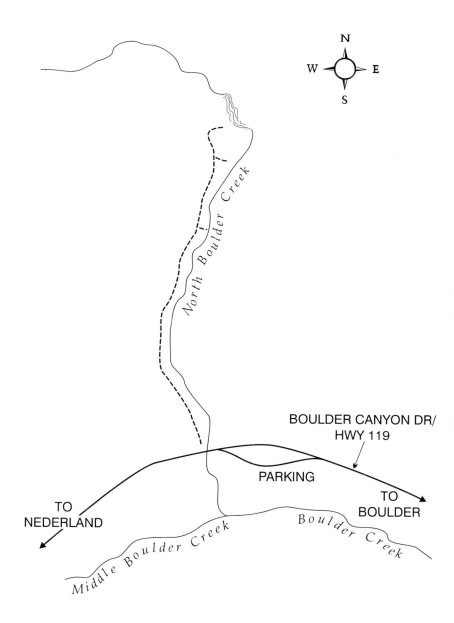

BOULDER FALLS

Hike 9
Lost Lake Trail

Hiking Distance: 4 miles round trip
Hiking Time: 3 hours
Elevation Gain: 1,000 feet
Topo: U.S.G.S. Nederland and East Portal

Summary of hike: This trail follows a dynamic stream of cascading water and small waterfalls. There are several creek and stream crossings (photo on page 18), views of the surrounding mountains, and a mountain lake at an elevation of over 9,000 feet.

Driving directions: From downtown Boulder, drive west on Canyon Boulevard. Canyon Boulevard turns into Boulder Canyon Drive/Highway 119 at the outskirts of town. Stay on this road for 16 miles to Nederland. Take Highway 119 south 0.7 miles to the Eldora Ski Area Road and turn right. Drive towards, then past, the town of Eldora to the trailhead parking area (5 miles). The last mile is gravel road.

Hiking directions: From the parking area, take the left fork to the trailhead. Cross the walking bridge over the North Fork of Middle Boulder Creek. Stay on the main trail one mile to the Lost Lake/King Lake junction. Along the way, listen for the sound of the raging water of the South Fork on the left. A short distance further are a magnificent cascades and falls. At the Lost Lake junction, take the bridge across the South Fork of Middle Boulder Creek and go to the left. A quarter mile further is the next junction. Take the left fork 0.5 miles to Lost Lake. (The right fork leads to the King Lake Trail, Woodland Lake Trail, and Devil's Thumb Lake Trail.) The Lost Lake Trail circles around the lake. To return, retrace your steps.

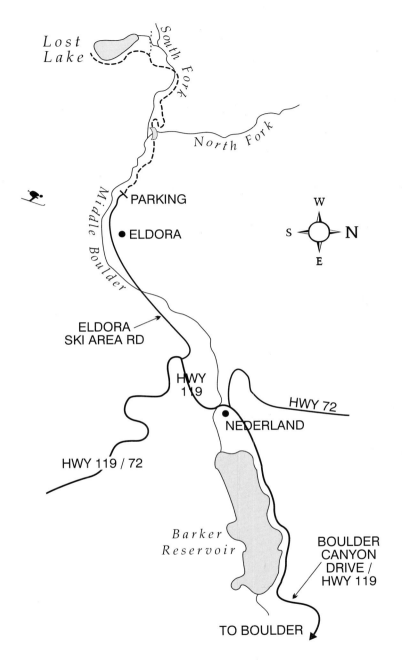

Lost Lake

South Fork

North Fork

Middle Boulder

X **PARKING**

● **ELDORA**

W
S ✦ N
E

**ELDORA
SKI AREA RD**

**HWY
119**

HWY 72

● **NEDERLAND**

HWY 119 / 72

*Barker
Reservoir*

**BOULDER
CANYON
DRIVE /
HWY 119**

TO BOULDER

LOST LAKE TRAIL

Hike 10
Chautauqua and Bluebell Mesa Trails
Chautauqua Park

Hiking Distance: 2.5 miles round trip
Hiking Time: 1.5 hours
Elevation Gain: 300 feet
Topo: U.S.G.S. Eldorado Springs

Summary of hike: Chautauqua Park has an excellent series of trails. This hike concentrates on two of these trails which make a loop. The hike has magnificent views of the town of Boulder and the Flatirons. The Flatirons, flat rock slabs resembling old-fashioned irons, are a prominent landmark in Boulder (back cover). These rocks are part of the same rock formation as in the Garden of the Gods in Colorado Springs and the Red Rocks Amphitheater near I-70. Another hike in Chautauqua Park is the Enchanted Mesa and McClintock Loop—Hike 11.

Driving directions: From downtown Boulder, take Broadway 1.5 miles south to Baseline Road. Turn right (west) and drive one mile to Chautauqua Park. Turn left and park in the parking lot next to the ranger station.

Hiking directions: From the parking lot, walk west to the trailhead. Follow the Chautauqua Trail through the meadow into the ponderosa pine forest towards the base of the Flatirons. A trail marker will direct you to the left at the Bluebell-Baird junction. Stay on the main trail to the Bluebell Mesa Trail; then take a left at the sign. This trail leads back to the Bluebell Road. Go left (downhill) back to your car.

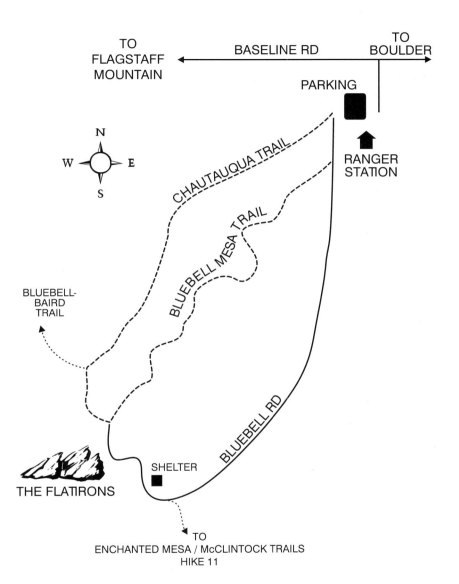

CHAUTAUQUA AND BLUEBELL MESA TRAILS

Hike 11
Enchanted Mesa and McClintock Trails
Chautauqua Park

Hiking Distance: 2.2 miles round trip
Hiking Time: 1.25 hours
Elevation Gain: 450 feet
Topo: U.S.G.S. Eldorado Springs

Summary of hike: The Enchanted Mesa Trail follows a fire road that gently climbs through a ponderosa pine and Douglas fir forest in Chautauqua Park. There are dramatic views of the Flatirons (photo on page 23), the city of Boulder, and the surrounding foothills. The return route is on the McClintock Trail, an interpretive nature trail with information stations about the climate, geology, plants, birds, and animals of the area. Another hike in Chautauqua Park is the Chautauqua and Bluebell Mesa Loop—Hike 10.

Driving directions: From downtown Boulder, take Broadway 1.5 miles south to Baseline Road. Turn right (west) and drive 0.7 miles to 12th Street—turn left. Continue 0.2 miles to the Chautauqua Auditorium parking lot on the right.

Hiking directions: The trailhead is behind the Chautauqua Auditorium by the southeast corner of the building. Take the fire road to the right, Enchanted Mesa Trail, uphill to the sign posted Mesa Trail. The Mesa Trail is also on the right, about 30 minutes from the trailhead. Follow the Mesa Trail downhill to the first posted junction on the right, the McClintock Trail. The McClintock Trail continues downhill until it intersects with the Enchanted Mesa Trail, completing the loop. Go to the right about 30 feet up the Enchanted Mesa Trail, and pick up the McClintock Trail again on the left. A short distance ahead is the trailhead and auditorium.

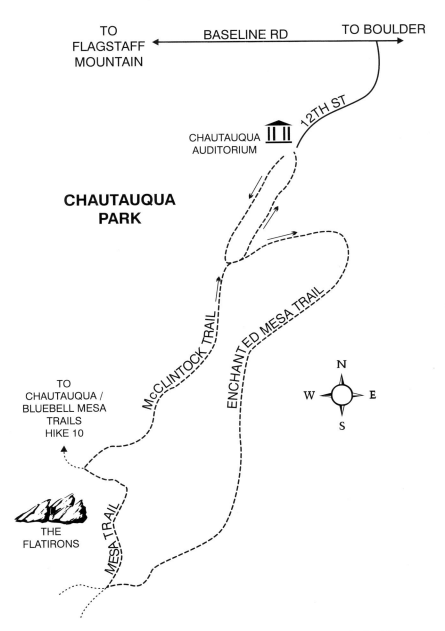

ENCHANTED MESA AND McCLINTOCK TRAILS

Hike 12
Amphitheater and Saddle Rock Trails
Green Mountain Loops

Hiking Distance: 1.5 miles round trip
Hiking Time: 1.5 hours
Elevation Gain: 700 feet
Topo: U.S.G.S. Eldorado Springs

Summary of hike: Three looped trails compose the Green Mountain Loops. The Amphitheater/Saddle Rock Loop is the shortest of the three. All are excellent hikes, although I have shown only the two nearest trails on the map. All three wind through the ponderosa pine and Douglas fir forest, with views of Boulder and the Flatirons.

Driving directions: From downtown Boulder, take Broadway 1.5 miles south to Baseline Road. Turn right (west) and drive 1.4 miles to Gregory Canyon. Turn left and drive up a short lane to the trailhead parking lot.

Hiking directions: The Amphitheater Trailhead is on the left (east) side of the parking lot. One hundred feet into this trail is a junction. Take the Amphitheater Trail to the right. (The left trail leads to the Chautauqua Park trails.) The trail is uphill using rocks and logs as a stairway. At about 3/4 mile, the Saddle Rock Trail intersects the Amphitheater Trail. Take the right fork downhill towards the parking lot. The left fork continues for a three-mile loop that returns through Gregory Canyon back to the parking lot.

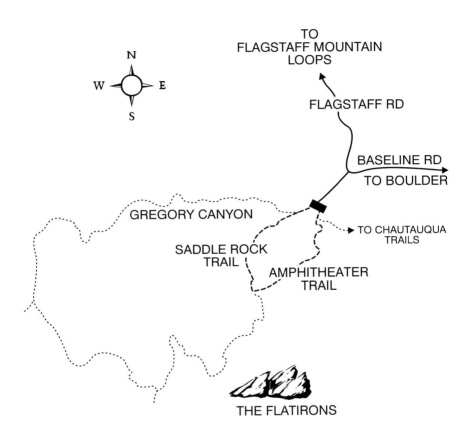

The Flatirons

AMPHITHEATER AND SADDLE ROCK TRAILS

Hike 13
Range View and Ute Trails
Flagstaff Mountain Loops

Hiking Distance: 1.5 miles round trip
Hiking Time: 1 hour
Elevation Gain: 300 feet
Topo: U.S.G.S. Eldorado Springs

Summary of hike: This hike follows a path around the west side of Flagstaff Mountain. This forested mountain has great views of the Indian Peaks and Longs Peak. The two trails that make this loop are part of a larger series of trails called the Flagstaff Mountain Loops. Two other trail combinations, the Chapman/Tenderfoot Loop, (just west of the Range View Trail) and the Boy Scout/May's Point Trail, are equally rewarding.

Driving directions: From downtown Boulder, take Broadway 1.5 miles south to Baseline Road. Turn right (west) on Baseline Road and drive 4.3 miles to the amphitheater turnoff to the right. Turn right and park.

Hiking directions: From the parking lot, walk north to the trailhead 100 feet ahead. Take the Range View Trail. About 0.5 miles further is the Range View/Ute/Boy Scout Trail junction. Take the Ute Trail to the right to complete the loop and return to the trailhead. The left trail at this junction is the Boy Scout Trail and leads to Artist Point and May's Point.

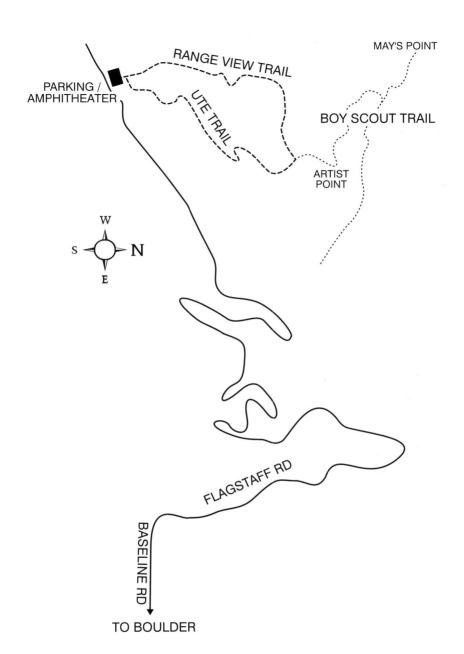

MAY'S POINT

RANGE VIEW TRAIL

PARKING /
AMPHITHEATER

UTE TRAIL

BOY SCOUT TRAIL

ARTIST
POINT

W
N
S
E

FLAGSTAFF RD

BASELINE RD

TO BOULDER

RANGE VIEW & UTE TRAILS

Hike 14
Meyers Homestead Trail
Walker Ranch Park

Hiking Distance: 5 miles round trip
Hiking Time: 2.5 hours
Elevation Gain: 600 feet
Topo: U.S.G.S. Eldorado Springs

Summary of hike: The Meyers Homestead Trail is located in the 3,778-acre Walker Ranch Park. It is a beautiful hike through open, rolling meadows covered with wildflowers and dotted with ponderosa pine and aspen trees. The trail follows a tributary of South Boulder Creek. At the trail's end is a scenic overlook of Boulder Canyon and Indian Peaks.

Driving directions: From downtown Boulder, take Broadway 1.5 miles south to Baseline Road. Turn right (west) on Baseline Road. Baseline Road becomes Flagstaff Road after leaving the city limits. Drive 8.2 miles along this steep, winding road over the top of Flagstaff Mountain to the Walker Ranch turnoff on the right. Turn right and park.

Hiking directions: From the parking area, follow the well-marked trail as it descends into the open meadow. At 0.5 miles is an old, deteriorated wood barn on the left with a trail leading towards it. The Meyers Homestead trail stays to the right. Continue to the trail's end for the magnificent views. To return, retrace your steps through the meadows back to the parking area.

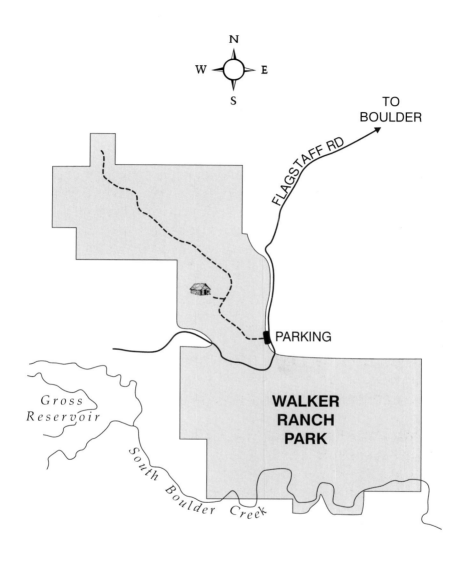

MEYERS HOMESTEAD
TRAIL

Hike 15
Homestead and Towhee Trails
Mesa Trails

Hiking Distance: 2 miles round trip
Hiking Time: 1 hour
Elevation Gain: 500 feet
Topo: U.S.G.S. Eldorado Springs

Summary of hike: The Mesa Trails trailhead is the beginning of a series of seven different trails. A favorite loop involves hiking in on the Homestead Trail and returning on the Towhee Trail. The trail crosses South Boulder Creek, has magnificent views of the Boulder Mountains, and returns through Shadow Canyon.

Driving directions: From downtown Boulder, drive south on Broadway 5 miles to Eldorado Springs Drive. Turn right and drive 1.8 miles to the Mesa Trails parking lot on the right side of the road.

Hiking directions: From the parking lot, walk west, crossing the bridge over South Boulder Creek. About 100 yards ahead, take the left branch onto the Homestead Trail. The trail junctions are marked. Homestead Trail follows the stream a short distance before heading up the hill toward the trees and a plateau. The trail then drops into beautiful Shadow Canyon. The Towhee Trail junction is in the canyon. Although you may continue further up by turning left at this junction, the Towhee Trail heads down canyon to the right. Complete the loop by returning to the trailhead.

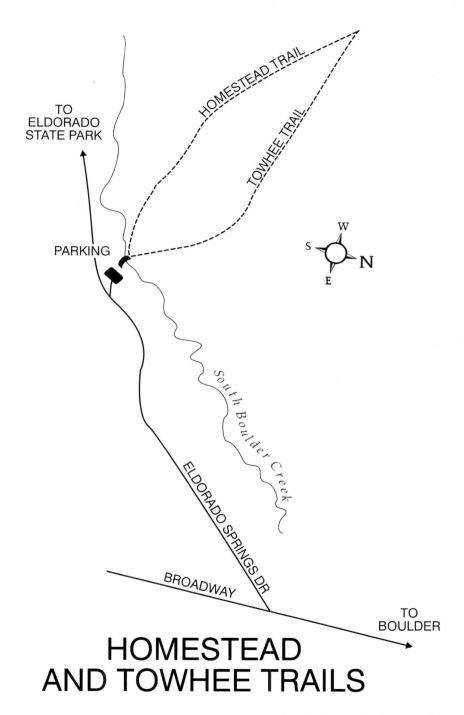

TO
ELDORADO
STATE PARK

HOMESTEAD TRAIL

TOWHEE TRAIL

PARKING

W
S ☉ N
E

South Boulder Creek

ELDORADO SPRINGS DR

BROADWAY

TO
BOULDER

HOMESTEAD
AND TOWHEE TRAILS

Hike 16
Fowler Trail
Eldorado Canyon State Park

Hiking Distance: 1 mile round trip
Hiking Time: 30 minutes
Elevation Gain: 100 feet
Topo: U.S.G.S. Eldorado Springs

Summary of hike: Eldorado State Park is incredible. South Boulder Creek swiftly tumbles through the canyon's sheer, red cliff walls that are 230 million years old. The winding road overlooks this splendor, making for a memorable day.

Driving directions: From downtown Boulder, drive south on Broadway 5 miles to Eldorado Springs Drive. Turn right and drive up canyon past the town of Eldorado Springs to the State Park—3.3 miles. There is a small entrance fee, and well worth it. From the park entrance, the Fowler Trail parking area is 0.7 miles on the left side of the road. The Visitor Center is 0.3 miles further and is located by a picnic area and the creek.

Hiking directions: From the parking area, the Fowler Trail begins to the left. Follow the trail as it overlooks the grand views of the canyon. The trail crosses two boulder fields, then curves to the right and out of the steep-walled canyon. From here, there are sweeping views across the Eldorado Valley and the city of Boulder. The trail continues through a forest and descends into Coal Creek Canyon. This is our turnaround spot. To return, retrace your steps.

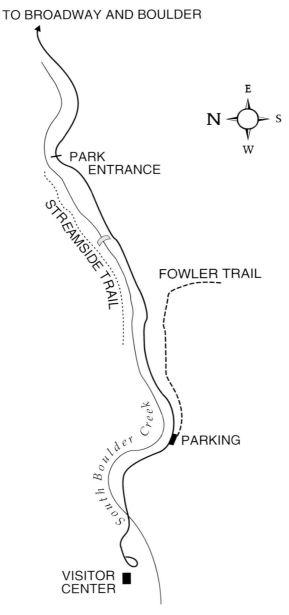

TO BROADWAY AND BOULDER

E
N
S
W

PARK
ENTRANCE

STREAMSIDE TRAIL

FOWLER TRAIL

South Boulder Creek

PARKING

VISITOR
CENTER

FOWLER TRAIL
ELDORADO CANYON

NOTES

Information Sources

Boulder Chamber of Commerce
2440 Pearl St.
Boulder, CO 80302
(303) 442-1044

City of Boulder Open Space
1101 Arapahoe Ave.
Boulder, CO 80302
(303) 494-2194

City of Boulder
Parks and Recreation
3198 Broadway
Boulder, CO 80304
(303) 441-3400

Boulder Mountain Park
Ranger Station
Chautauqua Park
P.O. Box 791
Boulder, CO 80306
(303) 441-3408

Colorado Parks and Recreation
1313 Sherman St.
Denver, CO 80203
(303) 866-3437

Boulder County
Parks and Open Space
P.O. Box 471
2045 13th St.
Boulder, CO 80302
(303) 441-3950

Boulder Convention and
Visitors Bureau
2440 Pearl St.
Boulder, CO 80302
(800) 444-0447
(303) 442-2911

Colorado Tourism Board
1625 Broadway Suite 1700
Denver, CO 80202
(800) 433-2656
(303) 592-5510

Colorado Parks and Recreation
1313 Sherman St.
Denver, CO 80203
(303) 866-3437

National Forest Service
(Boulder)
2995 Baseline Rd.
Boulder, CO 80303
(303) 444-6600

Nederland Visitor Center
P.O. Box 85
1st and Bridge St.
Nederland, CO 80466
(303) 258-3936

Eldorado Canyon State Park
Box B
Eldorado Springs, CO 80025
(303) 494-3943

Golden Gate Canyon State Park
3873 Highway 46
Rural Route 6 Box 280
Golden, CO 80403
(303) 592-1502

Other Day Hike Guidebooks

___ Day Hikes on Oahu $6.95
___ Day Hikes on Maui. 8.95
___ Day Hikes on Kauai. 8.95
___ Day Trips on St. Martin. 9.95
___ Day Hikes in Denver 6.95
___ Day Hikes in Boulder, Colorado 8.95
___ Day Hikes in Steamboat Springs, Colorado. 8.95
___ Day Hikes in Summit County, Colorado 8.95
___ Day Hikes in Aspen, Colorado 7.95
___ Day Hikes in Yosemite National Park
    25 Favorite Hikes 8.95
___ Day Hikes in Yellowstone National Park
    25 Favorite Hikes 7.95
___ Day Hikes in the Grand Tetons and Jackson Hole, WY. . . . 7.95
___ Day Hikes in Los Angeles
    Malibu to Hollywood 8.95
___ Day Hikes in the Beartooth Mountains
    Red Lodge, Montana to Yellowstone National Park 8.95

These books may be purchased at your local bookstore or they will be glad to order them. For a full list of titles available directly from ICS Books, call toll-free 1-800-541-7323. Visa or Mastercard accepted.

Please include $2.00 per order to cover postage and handling.
Please send the books marked above. I enclose $_____

Name _____

Address _____

City _____ State _____ Zip _____

Credit Card # _____ Exp. _____

Signature_____

1-800-541-7323

Distributed by:
ICS Books, Inc.
1370 E. 86th Place, Merrillville, In. 46410
1-800-541-7323 • Fax 1-800-336-8334

TOM EGENES

About the Author

The lure of the beautiful Rocky Mountains drew Robert to Red Lodge, Montana, in 1979. Hiking, exploring, and living in the Rockies has fulfilled a lifelong dream.

Robert Stone has traveled and photographed extensively throughout Asia, Europe, the Caribbean, Hawaii, and the continental United States.